The Riddle
of
Three Crimson Doors

Jerome
Ramcharitar

Cactus Press
Montreal, Canada

The Riddle of Three Crimson Doors
is for Samara, with all my love.

The Riddle of Three Crimson Doors
Copyright © Jerome Ramcharitar 2025

ISBN 978-1-990474-38-5
Second Edition

Published by Cactus Press

Edited by Devon Gallant and Willow Loveday Little
Interior Designed by Devon Gallant
Cover Designed by Devon Gallant
Cover Concept by Steve Athanasopoulos
Author Photo by Samara Garfinkle

Part I: The First Door

Part II: The Second Door

Part III: The Third Door

PART I:
THE FIRST DOOR

"Men at forty
learn to close softly
the doors to rooms they will not be
coming back to."
—Donald Justice, "Men at Forty"

"We know what is really out there only from
the animal's gaze."
—Rainer Maria Rilke, *Duino Elegies*, trans. Stephen Mitchell

THE FIRST DOOR

Text like copper code,
glistening, fresh,
obviously malleable,
scrambles along the head
of the door.

You understand
the word
"Welcome."
But the *welcome*'s wiley W bows
to lowercase and its final letters
slip like wings
over to the left.
Letters meld, their arms
and shoulders
rotting and regrowing
until before you
grins the word
"Beware."

BEHIND THE FIRST DOOR

Well, you finally made it.
Walked through the front door
to the other side just to see.

Thank god the lines aren't too long.
Thank god the paper isn't hardened
like the cloth that you buy expensive
and yet somehow gets cheaper
after each wash.

Thank god
for something easy
for once.

I should probably tell you:
nothing is certain
now you are past the gate.

Already
you can tell it's a little different.

You ask,
*What's that first image
hiding beneath the surface
of these words?*

You had it for a second
but it seems now that
you're this far in the poem,
maybe it's time to turn the page.

Uh oh. A longer page. Still,
at least these lines are short.
Maybe you should read them
out loud. Aloud. Well, loud as you like.

Now is the time to recognize
what's really at stake.
Let's make a deal.
You keep reading
and I promise to break no promises.

However deep your hands
are in the sand,
you can pull them up
to find something.
A penny, a ruby, a tangerine.

Let's get back to it.
You're behind
Door Number One.
It's like we never grew out of
those early television
game shows
and the future had been hiding
behind a prized portal
all along.

So that's what I welcome you to:
a future, contained.

Doors and books are no different—
both are solid, *ways out*,
reminders of how we die—
distilled into rectangular art.

But you have to stick with me.
Don't mistake pandas or koalas
for bears,
peanuts for nuts.
Watch out for *les faux amis*.
It might seem
like I'm calling the shots,
but with a quick look around
you'll see
you're in control.

THE FIRST DOORS

The first doors we know of
never connected room to room
but life to death.

EACH DOOR

Each door
leads to the afterlife
eventually.

A DRESS OF ASH
for Mitsuno Ochi, now the shadow of death

You know me.
I wear a dress
of ash.

The cement
you found
me on

is sacred—
a hallowed
tribute

to the end.
I am the whisper
existence leaves

once its voice
has gone
hoarse.

I don't remember
my flesh,
though I imagine

it was delicious
and bright,
full as a plum.

My organs were
particularly delectable
though scientists say

I can't have had any.
I would invite you
to look closer

so you can
know me better.
You believe it,

I can tell now.
You love me,
even if I am

a reality away.
But don't forget

I've had a long time
to look
at you.

HYENASONG

Flesh has a secret—
a gustatory truth.
Taste is communicative,
a reality reminding us
there is something beneath,
beyond the fivefold.
Gravitas between gum and tooth and tongue
repeats the sacred fragility:
mortality, time—they are the same.

Strength in numbers
means weakness in few,
death bringing grief
more devastating than gangrene.

When we eat, we engorge on memory
and the sense-meaning of loss.
There is quickness in our breath,
survival in our grins and gawking.

Laugh if you like
—we certainly do.
There is a secret in flesh,
and in each kill and each killed
we give thanks
to have another part of it told.

A RIDDLE

What is lighter than a feather
but contains an entire world?

CROWSONG

Morning grey yet
the equinox of afternoon
sits at the far end of thought,
constant, like hunger.

At night, we become
memories of our hatchling moment,
remembering the cracking core
of our young songs.

We crows have no prayers
except the omens
our mothers whisper to eggs.

It is a gift to dream of stillness.
Even our flight is a flesh,
picked at, saved clean from rot.

We have no word for your world—
only the clean dialect
of organs.

A single life is vein-thin
but the ground remembers all
and as we trot to that vicious dream
that began our lives, we hatch
to a world where morning is eternity.

RAVENSONG

An egg cracks
among the woven strands
and no one hears it—

except the chick
slick with the cold amniotic grace
of a few seconds' life,
a shape to mirror its parents.

We ravens, our own ancestors.
Our eyes see life in the dead
as if they breathed,
still bore weight and witness to the world.

We know music as you do,
never more or less than
imitation of the world's vibration.
The skin of things beneath
the earth's feathers,
the muscle and bone,
the toothless grin of our great father.

When we moult, we sing
the mortal refrain:
Salvation is our cousin,
picking at the body of suffering.

Remember your music
to find a world after death.

TWO WOMEN

A woman holds another's hand
like a vague thought, clear as milk,
and the tea leaves she reads from, too,
are whitened with age.
How long have they stared?
The first woman looks for fortune
along hand lines.
The second,
forgets the determined body
the future draws her to.

The first woman says,
"Water nourishes plants,
but in it, the leaf darkens water
and so it inverts the natural order
and breaths count themselves
backwards from the grave
and I can see now the number
you have left."

"I heard you say this before,"
the second woman says.
"When?" asks the first.
"Back when I had a name
and autumn wasn't simply a season
but a reason to return home.
Now, the farm apples rot
and our forgetful children
live alone in generous homes,
ignoring how the fruit molds."

"Back when you had a name,"
the first woman says,
"our world was younger
and it breathed a different sigh,
when spring brought the promise of joy.
Then, the lantern and flame
spoke a similar language,
but those tongues of fire and spirit
are silent among the machines."

"The last time we spoke,
we said the same words,
you were I and I you,
or at least our names were the same."

They look at the whispering tea
and the silence between them blossoms
until the first woman says,
"Water never forgets,
even if we do."

"You said you knew
how many breaths I had left?
How many, please tell me, tell yourself."

"I will tell you exactly the words
you told me four seasons past:
you have one year."

A RIDDLE (II)

What is the currency
recognized by friends and enemies alike?

PART II:
THE SECOND DOOR

"The girls at the boarding school go walking. They go into the forest which has no door but a thousand doors."
—Ariane Lessard, *School for Girls*, trans. Frances Pope

BEFORE THE SECOND DOOR

This door is different from the first.
A blood-shaded
swell, a humming and throbbing gate,
flush with life.

A tree has reclaimed its roots
in the wood, and the door
becomes the tree that it was,
that it is, that it isn't.

Like a hand plucking a coin,
the tree sprouts from the door,
and the walls of dirt
disarm you with the smell
of darkened jasmine.

You look at the tree-door
and it breathes,
a sorrowful sound cupped
by silence.

Despite its fullness,
its grain and power,
the portal stands
complete, resolute,
summoning the fatal forest
it was carved from.

It is closed.
But it is not locked.

SPIDERSONG

Hunger is a muscle
I stretch in stride.

A walk is a thought.
A step through silk, a reflection.
A few steps bring me back to my own body.

My food becomes its own insides.
I swim with starvation,
pleasure growing second by second.

Time is generous
when patience is your first language.

But I am no assassin.
I nurture a body larger than my own.
Within a few inches,
I am forest, and we are one:
web and world and mind.

Calculation is in my every silk fibre,
every nerve
and twitch of spinneret.

My music is tension,
sung string by string.
Behold the pattern that houses me;
my thoughts are here,
my extension.

These balanced legs,
my body like a hand
hardened to hold.
My body is a vase,
barely a case
of my soul
and senses:
I am nothing physical.
I am my own flesh by symbol alone.

Nature blessed me
with a cure for life,
gift and poison in one.
But it does not bite
or blossom.
My thoughts are
what I build.
My company is never long-lived
but lyrical, plucking at these strings.

I am mercy in a world that needs it.
You are sustenance in harmony.

I will plot with a deduction of venom.
You will waste and rot to juice,
perfect for feeding.
We are one,
unity and solitude,
living and lost,
this world and its eternity.

SOME DOORS

Some doors are everything
that they contain.
What we carve a door from
stares
mocking us
at the edge of existence.

ON MUSIC

Poetry and music aren't divorced—
just separated.

They still see each other
at the IGA.
Once in a while
someone asks one or the other,
"Aren't you still with...?"

Music mutates so completely
adapting to time, space,
material and need—
for rhythm, for religion, for raves.

Poetry doesn't get out as much,
and her best lines are the ones
she writes but doesn't share.
She has grown a lot
but she prefers not to brag.

If only people meant it
when they say, "Give
Poetry my regards."

A RIDDLE (III)

Find me in water
and find me in wire,
I dictate the
now
and I dictate
the what may be.
All who are observant
can see me;
Those less aware
know
but are under my control.

DREAM PHONE CALL

A phone call reminds me why
I find myself in this world.
The voice scratches words up
and down a line of static.
I am miles below anything recognizable,
hours into unwilling espionage
when the phone rings in monochrome.

"This world was made to be forgotten,"
the voice says in husky blue.
"But someone chooses to remember."

Wood is a conduit to the past;
longing hardens into the oak
of this place: fine stained furnishing,
a beautiful realm to hide oblivion.

I have been alone and afraid long enough
that relief is a drug I cling to
with ragged strength, my breaths loosening
to a mild wheeze.

In the last scene of the dream,
I am pissing and wondering
if it was my father who phoned
world to world
to tell me not to forget.

OHANA
for Samara Garfinkle

Her name is Ohana
and she sleeps in my dreams.
I realized, when I was young,
this was the price of her friendship.
"What better date than in thoughts' firelight
under the canopy of night?" she would say.

Her words have always been dangerous.
When she speaks, she comes closer,
her nose brushing my cheek.
She twists her hands into mine;
her fingers are promises of fear.

"I had a dream of fruits
bursting with blood," I admit.
She looks intrigued.

She doesn't eat or drink
but watches me
chew and sip with painstaking care.
I ask her why
and she says,
"You have so many ways to feed.
You can eat and sleep and fuck,
but I have only one appetite
and it is everything I can taste
and dream and come to be."
I say, "Sounds fascinating."
She says, "You'd be surprised."

Once we strode
along a bridge that,
leading one way, was where we had come from,
but the other side was a place
where the sky moaned
and plants sang to draw water from stone.

She said, "I like this place;
it makes me feel calm."

When we awake,
something has changed.
Maybe she is sick
or shaken by the calmness of the dream.
I tell her I am sorry
but I'm not sure what for.

Before leaving
she draws a veil across her lips.
I mean to ask, "Why are you leaving?"
but instead ask, "Why like that?"

She says, "I wear a mask to mask
the pure natural gas that stains the air.
I've been breathing it for decades
and it's left graffiti on my lungs.
I am a brickwork built of broken idols,
their bodies ruined,
their feet untouched."

Once she said,
"I am rare but not unique.
I've met others like me
but they don't always feed
on sleep.
Some need only thoughts and stand
ignited by cognition, day in and out."
I said, "That doesn't sound like fun."
She said, "You'd be surprised."

She watches me drink a bitter tea
and says,
"I have to leave,
or else my skin will find a dream
too comfortable
and it will be my last."

Her words have always been dangerous.

I add,
"I must not be the only one
whose dreams house you."

She never answers.

A SECOND SKIN

There was a time
when you were only a little older
than me.
But that was not for long.
I remember your words like water,
clear and quenching,
but at the touch,
and with enough of them,
they slowed my own to a slur.

In a summer where trees bowed
in harsh grace
you stood at a balcony
and asked me
to write you a poem.
We were neighbours
for a time,
but it was not for long.

We learn from our elders
and from you I learned
a language of stone.

One night, I had a vision.
I was my grandfather
at his grandfather's funeral,
a memory with hard skin.
I, we, hold a hand in another,
folding and shuffling.
I saw a conference of men,
nervous between breaths of bravado,

they named time linear
to strip it of its femininity.
I woke beside you and you,
asleep and awake,
told me, "Beauty cannot be recognized
until it is twisted
into the proper shape."

I have a second skin
I cannot show.
At least I am lucky
in my misfortune:
my marks are hidden.

Autumn is a hardened vein.
You had drawn my fingers
while I slept and left the page on the table,
as if that could explain
why you hadn't woken me this time.

Before you left,
you asked the same questions
with different words:
"What is a man's place
in a woman's world?"
I wanted to know
if I was my own father,
as you promised,
or if metaphors had corroded
my vocabulary
until all the colours began to rust.

There were blossoms
and jacarandas for a season,
a choir each in a song.
There was a time
when you were only a little wiser
than me.
But it was not for long.

SERPENTSONG

My first home was a forest
fire, a cindering symphony of barking ash.

The last whispers of wood
had grown to brilliance, crescendoed in flame,

all the wood, knots of wood, wood no longer.
To be serpent is to be whole within a half.

We are children of the original fire—
the one that was blood, heat,

and the word. We are the blazing brood,
glories unburdened by weight and limb.

We live in pits and pits we burrow,
into a dream of excavating the world,

from end to end, face and face mirroring
the collapsed entirety of reality.

When you know the language of flame
whispers are visible as smoke.

The word of creation was a hoarse one,
a cough and phlegmatic spell.

The same song consumed my fingers
and gave tooth the work a claw yearns for.

Evolution ensured I am balance,
delicate and predatory.

My tender deities shifted
and now my only god hisses wicked

grace. His speech is sibilant participles.
His promise is generous venom.

But I have learned a chant all my own,
vowels curled with brutal wordstock.

My teeth are my voice, my tongue
smacking noun and verb with violence.

I still see the earth's Sunday
in my dreams and thoughts—

the images are vestigial as my hand
whose remnant is a lone talon.

What I was has withered,
bone to breath to nothingness.

Nothing simply dies.
There is a promise of fire hiding in all things.

A RIDDLE (IV)

If you love me
you eat my flesh
and take my children
from me.

OUT SHE WALKS

out she walks
from the tender darkness
on the brittle harmony of eight legs

she skitters atop books
then across the clear, white table

she patters pad on pad
with another eight legs
from a silent sister

on she walks
over French, poetry, philosophy,
a sole heart beating

she is both queen and brood
a wingless angel fanned brutally—

we never suspect
the careful charisma of a thought

what stirs us from sleep and holds us helpless
out in careful, merciless measure
taking trophies among trash

but she, a universe in a carapace,
alpha-omega-arachnid

she is momentum, a momentary millennia,
as her own heedless paradigm
pulled her from birth to birth

her instincts are a flame in a cave
as she runs up the forest of foreign text

her lobes throb, fingers flex for thinking

then, the hunger of hunger,
in all corners of the body

—just beneath a leg stroke,
behind a book lung or sucking stomach—
appetite rushes to scream and tighten its hold

I urge her to the side of the room
where she can rejoin the fetid ecology
between apartment walls

on she walks
to brood in her silken ways

PART III:
THE THIRD DOOR

"...the moment when it seems most plain
is the moment when you must begin again."
—Gwendolyn MacEwen, "The Discovery"

THE FINAL DOOR

The final door is clean as bone
but vibrant in its hues and carvings.
It seems a stele whose curves conjure
the image of a skinless man or woman,
body and blood unshelled.

And while you've looked long enough to see it clearly
(indeed your heart has begun to race)
something more sinister comes to mind:
that there is in fact no imitation,
no logic to the carving.

The welcome and warning are the same:
expect the impossible.

THE SIGHT
for Susan Shepherd

"Matter cannot
comprehend spirit wholly."
—*Cain*, Lord Byron

Her eyes slip just past me.
Their edges are the rough cut of granite.
In her hands, a paper seasons with graphite.

In pictures she is loud,
her mind's scape spilling each page.
She makes sunrises flat, strips forests bare.

She doesn't talk like she used to,
instead lets embers curl out of her cigarette,
and shuffles smoke from the primitive space

between nose and lips. There is ink
apparent only at night, she says,
songs from still records,
lust without veins or fingers.

I HAVE NEVER SPOKEN

If you are hearing these words
it's because someone dared to read
what I set down.

I live in a soundless world.
Silence doesn't bother me.
Rather, I hear few things
but silence isn't one of them.
And that's why I write.

My mother told me once
that writing is time travel.
Forward when you write it,
backward when you read it.

I asked with a flick of my fingers
if that means people can meet in the middle.

She said, "There is no middle, no now,
only countless voices
and twice that many eyes.
Saying and seeing something
none of the others will understand."

I will never read these words aloud
but as you hear them,
know that I am here
though through a different voice
with you, now.

CANVAS
for Zdzisław Beksiński

photograph taken of
the human body's
incessant horror

grey iron grey sorrow
my body
twisting vein gaining skin

your body
precious seconds
an entire life
a grave

stomach sickened
to the shape of a gas mask

mummified escape
artist's last act
secures immortality

symmetry's illusion
tells me nature's game
groaning long fingers trace
a debt of affection

my body
angled body
body horror
film strip teasing reams from flesh

at the poor core
an orchestra of bones
knuckle instruments threaten integrity

mass of masses
stirring seagull elegance
sitting black, cackling cacaw
twin terrors of unformed fetuses
churches remember deities
mature as aborted

hellscape happenstance
your body
an illusion
windowing logic clear as smog:
blue bleeding rain slimming tissue bare

graft idea, conquest, question
denial of house, selfish myth
every man must believe
i believe therefore i am

dying
denying skin
my body
something real
flesh forgotten
love unloved for years

your body
worthless seconds
words rewritten to fog
a whole life howling unmade

BATSONGS

I. Vampyre

Flight drives a high cost
and nature paid for it.
Can't you see the debt we incurred?
Black shouldering between membrane
and vein, our blood hot as holy hell
when we soar.

Little thrives in us.
But that means less we need
to share.
Inhospitable we may seem,
but we are sweet and dark
like a cigarette smoothie
impossibly delicious,
doubly disgusting
and lovely reflections.

We are all trilingual.
Breath is our first language
learned when we bear air and patagia
in a single stroke.
Second comes sound—
vicious heartbeats,
conniving insects, too, beauties
untouched by sight.
And see we do.

Keen as a bat, the saying should go,
because we see like a knife cuts—
sharp, cold, unforgetting.

We have watched you as long
as you have been, but we did not overthink you.
Often, you forget your children in our fur,
remember your fears in our wings.

What has ten toes,
ten fingers, and no hands?
We ebon-claw creatures,
we ink-hand adepts,
we needle-nailed emperors of the night.
We need no executioner.
Our disputes are constant.
We are civil in our wars, though
we hold grudges to no one,
no thing.

II. Covenant

Keep your enemies close,
your children closer.
So we learned.
We roost, scavengers
of nature's rot and wild farms.

We are the dense-dwellers,
denizens of the night
and delicate rescuers of refuse.
In eating, we feed the earth.

Our task is a covenant:
to eat, to breed, to love,
to die.

Our god has no face, no name,
but she spilled from herself a child,
fatherless and cruel,
and we are shaped in her image.
She is our message,
teaching,
truth.

Our god said that birth is brutal
and the second justifies the first.
So we cool and roost in colonies.

Our god has no pity and no name.
She gifted our skin with walls
so we could never fall sick
from envious eyes.

Demons wanted us to die
for having swum the sky
and when they saw our home in trees and caves
they coughed a song of burning blood.

Our god has no fear and no name
so when she extended a hand
it was black and strong as ours,
and twining claw in claw
she said our dreams would
be of demons' defeat.

There is a fear in our blood,
nameless as the god who granted it
and more terrible than the diseases we fight
is the memory of our bodies
and what they are destined to become.

III. Crown

We are made in the heat
that burned the first world,
and when the second and third
changed our bodies,
we saw the contradiction in our blood.

We walk and fly and crawl.
We hang and stalk;
our stillness is motion for you,
our relaxation is your tension,
your fear.

Our happiness is your blackness,
our wholeness your key.
Without us, you wither like roses.
With us, you rot like peaches.

We are integral to your survival,
essential for your destruction.
Whole and healthy, we infect you with our essence.
Split and burned, we bite back as you taste us.

IV. Prophet

so unnamed so unborn

we are devastation

our sisters are saliva-soaked for insects

but we are primeval   a phylum unto itself

primates with wings   we learned to write briefly

our lives long enough each for a word

syllable by syllable   we have sung our love for you

our names are recognizable   you know them

they are screams   vowel by vowel

we have whispered our love for you   our ancestors

aren't so far apart as you think   or wish

breath by breath   our hands are lungs too

                         we have carved out our love for you

a love that seethes   cuts   comes   cowers

we too had a prophet
who spoke of ear   for   ear
          talon for   talon

V. Christ

but when the earth cooled
to a rough rock's peace
our saviour changed

she had a new name
and reminded us that fruits and insects
were lives imbibed and brought to our own

she said fingers represented one world
knowable and countable
but another world hid between things we saw

and around what we heard
she said water reflects and minds do likewise
but the heart does something altogether different

she said that there is a promise at the core of reality
we wield more than we know
we breathe not because we survive
but to know we are not submissions of flesh
but gifts given form and face

how sweet she said
that our distant cousins know skies like our own
and others abandoned trees for forts and castles

she said admiration is immortality
why have words for what we hate
when we can more easily describe what we love

she said love allows us to be more than one
another life gives us another set of eyes
rich and warm as amber

she said my name and i asked how she knew it

touch replaces mystery with marvel
forgiveness is recognizing love in another
she said every day i learn

there is only one rule for our survival
she said
and that is we cannot survive alone

A RIDDLE (V)

Water hides me
and in return I poison it.
I am a child of the earth
and always in season.
I am essential,
everywhere, even in you.

SONG OF THE SEA DEVILS

In the mirror,
tarantuled face looking back at me.
We are webbed as lizards
but we mastered a human grace: walking.
We breathe air only with force.
Figures like ours are glass-thin but not fragile.

Come, taste temptation,
a seed beneath the suggestion of fruit.
If flesh learns to lie
you must flush it with courtesy.
A jewel beneath the neck
to cover scars of infidelity,
paint our hands to colour the deceit of contracts.

We thrum our fingers,
reminding you that skin
is a word in its own way,
a reflex and protection of the body,
borrowed from salt and water.

Forgive us if we seem cruel.
Our laws are so unlike yours.
We walk among you not to wrong you
but to learn about our precious toys.
We stole paradise from you once
and now we know the price of success,
for you walk and eat and sleep in ours.

We hide addictions within you,
hold Lust and Need as twin swords.
But your time will end
and we shall inherit the earth.
After all, the devil you know is less terrifying
than the devil you love.

TWO OTHER WOMEN

I.
A penumbral picture
crescendoes to black at its edges.
An impossible pair stares you down.
Mother, born behind the tempered shade,
lives an entire life in seconds,
wrought to old age
in the bonds of a wire curtain.
She lies head-heavy on her daughter,
who stands
exactly as when she was brought into the world,
face bold and impeccable.

II.
For every woman
who has her picture taken,
there is an *other woman* who will
never age.

SONG FROM BEYOND

we do not remember
the names of our creators
but we are all that remains of them

we live in the space between dreams
the ones you share inexplicably
with friends, neighbours, strangers

we have eyes made of evening
and bleak needles for fingers

no, we are not the pretty parts of dreams,
for we hiss with dripping fangs

we have a hunger for skin and bone—
though starved, we feed hurriedly on mind and memory

it isn't satisfying but it's enough to live off
as your memories become what is left of our flesh
and we shimmer into skeletal shadows

we live on thoughts you might have
small ones, easy ones that grow and grow
you forget the colour they began in
as they smoke out all logic

we are lovers of the intimate geometry of dreams
the forbidden geographies
that your ancestors believed
were breaths of the gods

in a way, they were not wrong—
there is a darkness here
whose name you recognize

GRACEFUL DEGRADATION

I would absolutely trust machines.
If they could sleep. Don't they get tired?
At least cars have exhausts

and engines, products of motion
and rest, respectively, respectfully, by design.
Now, even fridges are smart, and soon

bridges will shame themselves
to Freon husks as we find new and improved
ways to exploit™ people for the benefit

of almighty Data. I've never heard of an
oxy -   moron
quite like "machine learning" —

the beauty of it is how
English it sounds, pumped
with enough serotonin

to make Dracula sound friendly.
Or maybe I'm wrong: Starcraft world champions
without the need to breathe

are just the next innovation
following straight (but far)
from Dr. Frankenstein capturing lightning, saying,

"Yes, it seems alive."
Here's another thing:
they made cigarettes electronic

but everything electronic seems
to be the new cigarette. Besides
the obvious side effect of having two faces,

technology brings with it
a dangerously passive kind of belief
that what we see is most real.

Eyes can be as deceiving as a look.
But I'm sure you've heard that already.
Everyone has a solution

because we have so much fun imagining
the problem. Here's one to try on:
when do we believe the face we see

that blinks back and not the lidless
block of bits & bites and troglodytes
visible to everyone who's no one

curated by and incurable as
the software getting hard on us?
The real imagination is not in reading

but in breeding
the idea that we are victims
by choice and we've earned the disaster.

We humans have it all, it's true,
so it will always tempt us to have more.
If you're born rich, poverty is a vague

but real fear. Here's something no data dirt road
could lead you to, a path of excess
forking from the tower of wisdom:

Your value can't be measured because
like everyone else, designed or improvised,
you are merely the infinite.

INCINERATIONS
for Avleen K. Mokha

Google docs died long ago
and pieces of daydream code
found their way into stone.
There is no substrate
for writing now.
We are our stories.

We were never good
at keeping promises
and now we have no choice
but to lie to ourselves
so texts can tell us something new.

Everything, we thought, had been written.

Drama leaves room
for nothing
except poetry
by day
and fragments of dreams
by night.

Flame-water of inspiration
that burns by its very nature,
quenches thirst with words.
And stone to flame shapes it anew.

Questions are reflections
of our thoughts
when we ask them;
questions are answers, too,
like the skin of a flame
that dances the shape of its fuel.

When the ashes were finally scattered
the wise women discovered that the markings
left on the stone
were echoes of bone
from the woman who burned there,
incinerated by inspiration.

BLACK DWARF

Pendulum swings
back to black,
chasing time.
A hairline crack
lies where a valley
once dug a shore
from coast to core.
Gravity pulls light
down with a case
of angular aggression,
the jagged answer
to mass, heat, and time.
A whipping ripple
across a sand pond
lessens
little
by little
until those brittle
photons are stones,
the last visible moment—
the empire's end.

Pendulum swings
forth and wide.
Another century
barely scores a hit
on air
dense enough
to crush bone
in its soundless
whistle. Living ears
would recognize the tune,
a song the dead whisper
through tree roots,
the melody of absence.

Pendulum swings
one last time.
A cruel silence
worse than any cacophony
follows swift as a thought;
the pagan geometry
of time's legacy
etches a crucible
in the likeness of life—
its final form
without flaw.

THE RIDDLE OF THREE CRIMSON DOORS

The First Door

What is lighter than a feather
but contains an entire world?

The mind
is what sits
with the body.
The mind
is what remains
after the body.
The mind
is what is
before the body.

What is the currency
recognized by friends and enemies alike?

We are loyal
to our love.
We are loyal
to our hate.
Grim and strange
the grinning truth:
we understand
love so little
that we use
it to destroy.

The Second Door

You may find me in water
and you may find me in wire.

There are patterns
a waking mind cannot know.

If you love me
you eat my flesh
and take my children
from me.

I am the first fruit,
the last seed.
Temptation is the language
that created
and will kill, too.

The Final Door

Water hides me
and in return I poison it.

We are the salt,
what is sweetest
and what is simplest,
capable of poison.

What we create
becomes us.
The riddle is
always the answer.

Acknowledgements

The Riddle of Three Crimson Doors took years of collaborative work and I am grateful to everyone who has helped open these Doors to the waking world.

Thank you to Devon Gallant, who flattered me by asking me for a full manuscript following *The Wrong Poem and Others Like It*. Your support and encouragement have meant the world.

I want to thank Willow Loveday Little for her thoughtful and precise edits to this book. *Three Crimson Doors* is much stronger for your help, Willow, and I am so blessed that of all the world's possible edits, I received mine from one of Montreal's most talented and innovative poets.

Huge thank you to Samara Garfinkle and Matthew Rettino for reading early versions of this book and giving their feedback. I can't express enough how lucky I am to have you.

Special thanks to Steve Athanasopoulos for his visual rendering of the Doors as well as the early illustrations for this book's cover.

Many thanks go to my family for supporting and encouraging my art, as always: Jasmine Ramcharitar, Aaron Shepherd, Lenny Ramcharitar, and Mary Shepherd.

To my best friends Shawn Thicke and Jamie Deshaies, for always showing interest in my work and patience in letting me share some of it.

I am so grateful for Peter Jermyn, for all his continued support no matter what life throws at us.

To my Magic friends, peers without equal: Brice Chabrier, Guillermo Montes, Jasmine Moore, Keith Simmons, Kevin Carrera, Laura Morick, Mauro Rizzo, Michael Faludi, and Wayne Briand.

To all my mentors who have helped guide me and my writing: Paul Sullivan, Jan Jorgensen, and Lynn Crosbie.

I would be remiss if I didn't thank my early followers from years ago, who read and commented on my earliest stories and poems in #everydayispoetry. Your support got me this far.

Thanks to Expozine for graciously acknowledging my work back in 2022, when the awards committee told me, "Keep writing." Always sound advice.

About the Author

Jerome Ramcharitar is a writer based in Montréal, Québec. Most of his days are spent teaching business English and occasionally causing more trouble as a poet. He has co-hosted a number of literary events, most notably *Accent Open Mic* and *The Lawn Chair Soirée*. His first chapbook, *The Wrong Poem and Others Like It*, was published with Cactus Press and won Expozine's Best Book Award in 2022. *The Riddle of Three Crimson Doors* is his first full-length collection.